A Kettle of Hawks

TO JIM AND DOTTY BRETT,
two who have dedicated their lives
to the preservation of the wild.

LOTHROP, LEE & SHEPARD BOOKS

NEW YORK

JIM ARNOSKY

A Kettle of Hawks

and other wildlife groups

Printed in the United States of America.

First Edition 1 2 3 4 5 6 7 8 9 10

Library of Congress Cataloging in Publication Data
Arnosky, Jim. A kettle of hawks and other wildlife groups/ written and illustrated
by Jim Arnosky.
p.   cm. Reprint. Originally published: New York: Coward, McCann & Geoghegan, 1979. Summary: Discusses six animals that form groups, including a swarm of bees, colony of ants, and kettle of hawks. ISBN 0-688-09279-9. — ISBN 0-688-09280-2 (lib. bdg.)   1. Animal societies—Juvenile literature.   [1. Animal societies.   2. Animals—Habits and behavior.]   1. Title.   QL775.A76   1990   591.52'4—dc20.
89-12459 CIP AC

Many of the names we use for groups of animals describe something interesting about the animals in each group. These names can be a starting point for learning more about wildlife.

JIM ARNOSKY
Ramtails 1990

A Kettle of Hawks

Hawks silently soaring,
circling, climbing,
high in a kettle of hot air.
A Kettle of Hawks in the sky.

Hawks fly alone much of the time, but in autumn and spring some travel great distances together. These seasonal movements are called migrations. To save energy, hawks will soar along using air currents or columns of hot air called thermals. The hot air in a thermal pushes the hawks high in the sky, giving them the altitude they need to peel away and glide for miles farther on their migration course.

When many hawks circle upward in the same thermal, they are said to be "kettling," because it looks as though the birds are boiling in a great kettle of air.

A Swarm of Bees

Bees in a ball—
humming, buzzing,
resting on a limb, then flying again,
following their queen to begin a new hive.
A Swarm of Bees in the orchard.

All activity in a beehive revolves around the queen bee. She is the mother of the hive, laying thousands of eggs that hatch into more bees—workers, drones, even new queen bees.

The worker bees are females. They gather pollen from flowers, bring it to the hive, and make it into beebread and honey. Worker bees also produce wax to make honeycomb.

Drones are male bees. They do not do any work. Drones mill about the hive, eating, growing fat, until one of them is singled out to mate with the queen. When that drone is chosen and mating is done, all the drones are driven from the hive. Since drones cannot feed themselves, they starve.

When the hive becomes overcrowded or a young queen takes control from an old queen, the bees will swarm. They leave the hive suddenly and go off, following one queen, to begin another hive in a new place. A swarm may contain thousands of bees—a buzzing cloud drifting through the air.

A Colony of Ants

Ants in a line,
busy, working,
carrying food down their hole.
A Colony of Ants under the sidewalk.

Ants live in highly organized communities called colonies. A colony may number from one dozen ants to more than half a million. Every ant in the colony has a specific part to play in the community. There is a queen to produce the colony's young, there are drones that live only long enough to mate with the queen, and there are workers and soldiers.

Ants eat all types of food. Most of it is found or scavenged and stored underground. A favorite food is the honeydew produced by another insect, the aphid. Some ants in the colony farm aphids, keeping small flocks and "milking" them of their honeydew. If you live in a village or town, farmers nearby supply your home and school with milk. The ant farmers supply honeydew for the rest of the colony.

Whenever I find a colony of ants, I watch closely to see if I can tell which ants are the soldiers protecting the colony from intruders and which ants are the builders keeping pathways clear and digging new tunnels. I look for ant farmers tending their aphid flocks.

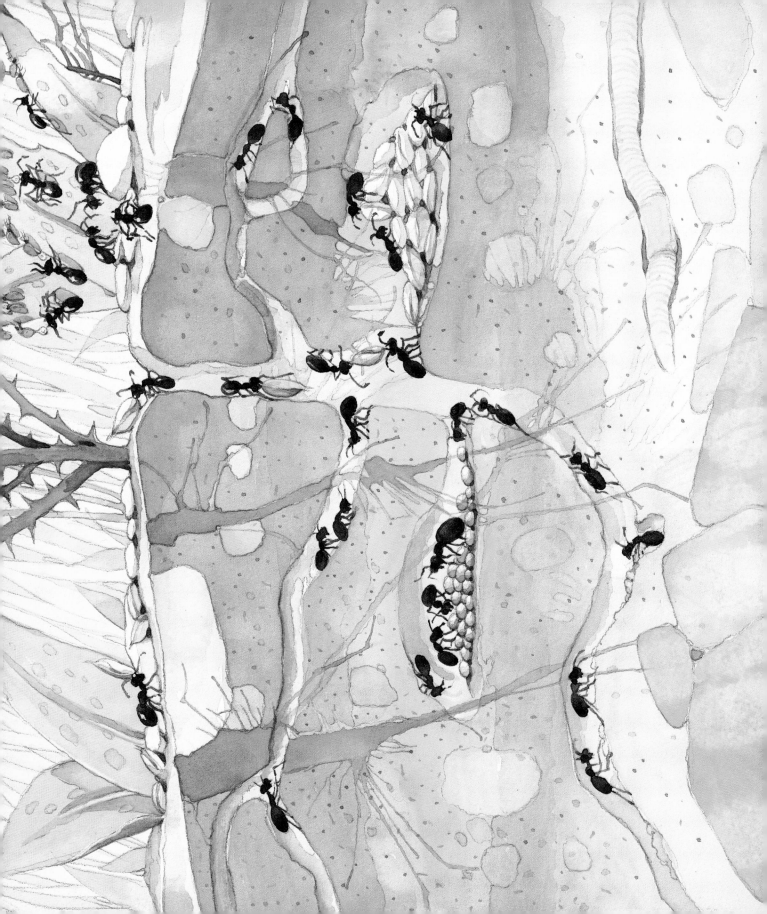

A School of Fish

Fish swimming,
darting together,
waving their fins in the water.
A School of Fish in the lake.

Minnows, bass, herring, and many other species of fish swim and feed in groups called schools. Imagine a group of classmates on a school trip, all facing in the same direction, staying close together. This gives you an idea of what a school of fish looks like underwater.

In the underwater world there is safety in numbers. A school of small fish may seem like one large fish to an enemy. Also, by grouping together, individual small fish are harder to locate than if they swam scattered all over.

Some species of fish swim in schools when they are very young and tiny and swim separately after they have grown bigger. Other species swim in schools all their lives.

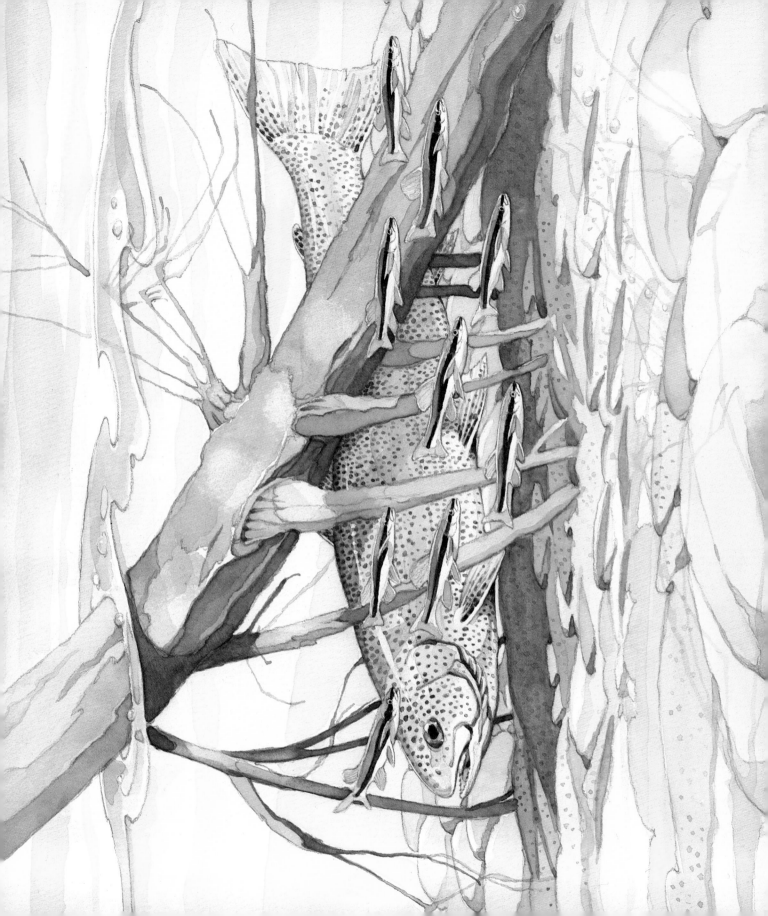

A Cloud of Tadpoles

Hundreds of tadpoles,
tiny black specks,
scattering as you approach.
A Cloud of Tadpoles in the shallows.

For most of the year toads live solitary lives on land. In spring they migrate to nearby water to mate. The female deposits her eggs in the water in a long string of clear gelatin. Inside the string are tiny black eggs.

After mating, the toads return to land and resume their solitary ways. The strings of eggs are left floating in the water. The eggs hatch into tiny tadpoles that look like black dots with short wiggly tails. The tadpoles stay together close to shore, where they feed on algae and other underwater plants.

When a group of tadpoles are startled, they dart downward and burrow into the soft bottom of the pond, stirring up the mud and silt and creating a brown cloud in the water.

As the tadpoles get bigger, metamorphosis takes place. The tadpoles grow front and hind legs. Their gills are replaced by air-breathing lungs, and their tails get smaller. Soon the tadpoles are tiny toads, ready to hop out of the pond and begin living on land.

A Gaggle of Geese

Geese in the distance,
honking, squawking,
landing in groups on the lake.
A Gaggle of Geese on a sandbar.

Even after a long journey geese are full of energy, flapping their wings, honking and gaggling noisily to one another. They are in top physical condition before, during, and after migration. This is due to their energy-saving system of flying in drafts. The leader of the flock breaks a trail through the air, and the rest of the geese follow behind. Each goose, flying a little to the side and rear of the goose ahead of it, is sucked along in the strong draft of air caused by the V-shaped flight formation. By "drafting" and taking turns leading the flock, the geese are able to pace themselves and conserve energy all through their long migration. And wherever they land, in a large flock or small groups called gaggles, they are never too tired to honk up a good goose conversation with their fellow travelers.

The next time you hear a name used to describe a group of animals, wonder about it. Find out if the name tells you something about the nature of the animals themselves. Anything you learn will add to the fun of watching wildlife.

Here are some other animal groups you can think about:

A Bed of Clams   A Pod of Whales

A Paddle of Ducks   A Brood of Chickens

A Band of Coyotes   A Beaver Colony

A Wolf Pack